GARDENS ILLUSTRATED

KNOW HOW

PROPAGATING

NEW PLANTS FROM OLD

by

PENELOPE HOBHOUSE

JOHN BROWN PUBLISHING

FOREWORD

Most gardening techniques are very simple and can be discovered by using common sense and imagination. Getting the soil right is the first priority. Good, well-prepared tilth with plenty of earthworms is obviously going to give plants a good start. If the worms are happy plants will probably thrive. Planting correctly is another essential. This includes choosing plants with well-developed root systems, and avoiding those which have been badly grown or are pot-bound. Each plant or group of plants must have the right soil and climatic conditions. It is no use planting acid-loving plants in alkaline soil or planting the moisture lovers where they will dry out.

Established woody plants need pruning and training, often on an annual basis, and most soft-stemmed perennials need dividing in order to maintain their vigour. The most fun in gardening comes from making new plants from old; propagating from cuttings and growing newplants or replacements from seed.

Gardening carefully and thoughtfully brings its own rewards. The pleasure of watching things grow, waiting patiently, not hurrying results, that is the best way to gain experience. Like the garden itself, gardening know-how grows with time.

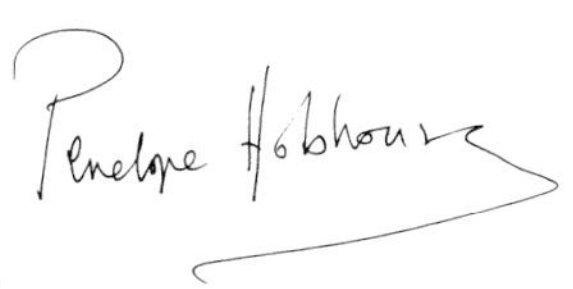

Marian Hill

I enjoy `making' plants more than all the other tasks in the garden, but, although fairly successful, I can still have spectacular failures. However, gardeners learn as much from failures as from successes and an enormous part of the pleasure in learning how to produce new plants from old is in the excitement of experimenting. I have been germinating seeds and rooting cuttings for years, just enough to produce certain sorts of plants for my own garden, not at all a professional operation. Like most home gardeners, I muddle along, producing a limited number of plants either for replacement and renewal or for temporary seasonal displays. It is never easy and I'm learning all the time.

I have always wanted to grow most of my own annuals from seeds or cuttings. Now, because I am away a lot and germinated seeds need regular attention during the vital after-care period, I sow only the seeds of those plants it is difficult to get at my local nursery. I also take cuttings of tender plants and shrubs grown as annuals, which are an essential part of my gardening schemes. Cuttings need less daily care than seedlings and are less likely to be damaged by swings of temperature in spring.

COLLECTING SEEDS FROM PLANTS

Growing plants from seed is never more exciting than when you have taken the seed from your own garden. Collecting seeds is enjoyable, but should only be done on a dry, sunny day, never directly after rain when the seeds will be sodden. Seed is usually ready for collection when brown or black and crisp. If seed is picked green, dry it off in full sun on a windowsill. It is normally only worth taking seed from species that will come true. Many annuals that are known as F1 hybrids (two true breeding species crossed to produce a hybrid often more vigorous than either parent) will not produce seed that germinates to make a worthwhile plant the following year.

The quickest method of collection is to cut off flowering heads and put them upside down in large

COLLECT SEEDS FROM THE GARDEN when ripe into dry paper bags. Often it is easier to cut off the whole truss or flower head and clean and sort the seeds later. Do this on a dry sunny day rather than when the air is damp. Even on the driest day, do not use polythene or plastic bags because any residual moisture on the plants may make the seeds slightly damp and in plastic they will rot.

envelopes or paper bags - don't use polythene or plastic bags because the seeds may still be slightly damp and will rot. Hang the bags in a dry airy place and shake occasionally so that the seeds fall into the bottom. Cleaning and teasing seed out of dead petals or protective covers takes little time and, unless you are selling the seed, can be done very quickly. When completely dry and clean, seeds can be stored in a dry place. Alternatively, put them in sealed plastic envelopes in a container with some silicone gel added to absorb moisture and prevent rotting. Store the envelopes in the fridge until it is time for sowing the seeds.

HANG FLOWER HEADS upside down in a dry shed with circulating air. Sort the seeds in winter or before sowing.

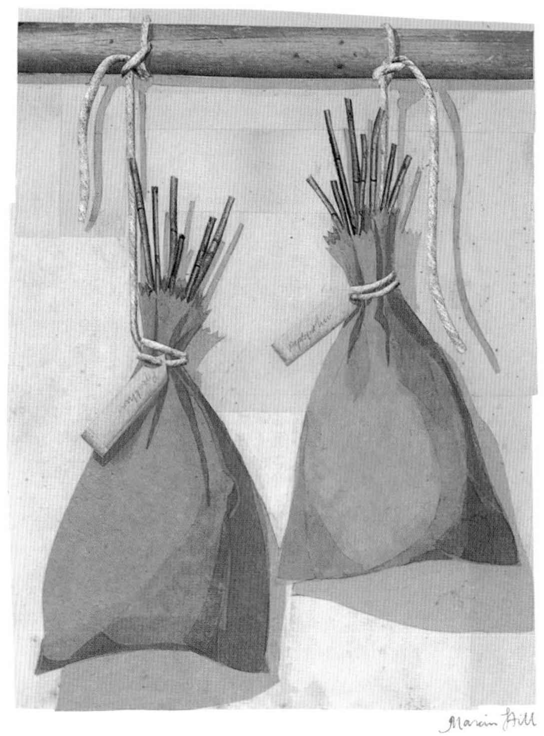

Seed of most annuals, biennials and perennials are stored over winter and sowing takes place in February, March or April. Some perennial seed, however, including hellebores, cyclamen, anemones, lilies and snowdrops, does not store. The seeds should be left on the plant until they are mature, just before natural dispersal. As soon as they are ripe they need sowing in pots or trays and to be kept in a cold frame or greenhouse. They are pricked out in the normal way.

Fruits that contain seed capsules need breaking open and the seeds dried before they are sown. Seeds from woody plants are often difficult to germinate. Ripe in the autumn they have in-built dormancy (a chemical inhibition to embryo development) which prevents germination until the onset of favourable conditions. These conditions can involve a period of cold after sowing; placing the tray or pot in a refrigerator for a few weeks and then giving artificial heat will encourage germination. Dormancy tables in any reliable propagation book will be a helpful guide. Other woody plant seeds have a thick seed-coat which prevents water being taken up. Soaking in hot or even boiling water will encourage germination. In fact many larger seeds such as those of sweet peas, and most of the woodies, can be soaked in warm water for a few hours before sowing to improve results. Some seed capsules, usually from countries with hot climates, can be placed in a hot oven and will then split open to reveal the seed.

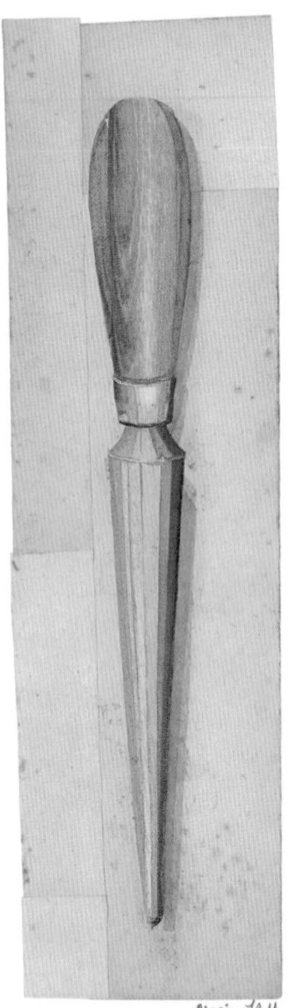

GROWING FROM SEED

I used to start my seeds as the days lengthened in February. I found that after pricking out into trays or pots, the seedlings still required weeks of protective heat in a greenhouse before going into cold frames in April. Also, having formed spreading root systems early on, they needed constant re-potting before being planted out in May. The process was lengthy and labour intensive, requiring a great deal of care and attention as well as time. So now I sow seeds in mid-March, and find they do just as well, quickly making up time by faster growth as days lengthen.

A DIBBER with an almost pointed wedge shape is an ideal tool for making holes for larger seeds or seedlings in trays.

You don't need a lot of expensive equipment to germinate seeds. Seeds need water, oxygen, a good compost and a suitable temperature in order to start growth - and seedlings once germinated, need light and air. I use a plastic tray with a tight-fitting (but vented) transparent lid, and heated cables in the base which can sit on a window-sill or a greenhouse shelf. Even simpler, after sowing, is to place the trays inside air-tight plastic bags, or under a transparent film, until the seed germinates. Given the right conditions, each seed will awake from protective dormancy and put out a shoot and a root system. Seeds need high humidity to germinate, but need fresh air as soon as the leaves are formed or else they will rot, so take the trays out of the plastic bags as soon as the seeds 'green-up'.

The compost you use for sowing needs to provide adequate aeration and sufficient water-holding capacity. It should be of a neutral type, that is neither acidic nor too alkaline, with a pH reading of about 6.4 (which you can, if necessary, check with a pH kit of the same type you would use to ascertain the pH level of your garden soil). You can make your own compost mix from sterilised soil, but this is very labour-intensive and not worth the effort unless you produce plants commercially. For sowing, I buy a peat-based seed compost (you can use a peat-free, soil-less equivalent). I fill seed trays to the brim, firm down the compost and hold them down in water until they are saturated. I then spray the surface with a fungicide, and plant the seeds the next day.

Different seeds need slightly different treatment

at sowing time. Some usually the finest, simply need pressing into the surface of damp compost and covering with glass or a plastic bag to conserve moisture and heat until the first shoots appear. Seeds which require full light for germination include antirrhinum, matthiola(stock), nicotiana (tobacco plant).

I grow a lot of salvias from seed - mostly the blue forms. Although light is recommended for germination of salvias, and it is advised to sow them on the surface, I find that a 3 mm (1/8 in) covering layer of perlite on the surface of the compost allows enough light to penetrate while keeping the soil adequately moist.

Other seeds germinate in the dark, covered completely with compost. The general rule seems to be that the thickness of the layer of finely-sieved compost covering the seed should be three or four times the size of the seed itself. Very small seeds can be mixed with fine silver sand to get a more regular distribution and eliminate tight bunches of seedlings appearing which are all too easily damaged in the pricking out stage.

Large seeds, and those that dislike transplanting, at pricking out can be sown in individual 75 mm (3 in) pots, which may be either plastic or degradable peat. Seedlings germinating in plastic containers need transferring to a larger size pot when the fibrous roots expand to fill the original pot, while those in peat can be planted inside a larger pot or directly into the ground. Peat pots, when planted, must have their rims covered with soil or the whole pot dries out when exposed to air with disas-

SEEDLINGS SHOULD BE individually picked out into pots or a deep tray. Fingers are as good as tools for this delicate work. Lift the seedling by the leaves, using a fork or widger, a small hollow tool, if necessary, to prise it out. Never handle them by their fragile stems. Prepare a hole, using a dibber or a finger. Drop the seedling very gently in the hole and lightly firm into the compost.

trous consequences. I sow salvias, sweet peas, cerinthes and any leguminous plant, as well as any individual shrub or tree specimens, in peat pots.

Keep the seed trays or pots at a regular temperature of between 18° and 21° Centigrade (65° and 70° Fahrenheit). As soon as germination begins, give the seeds more light and air, though not too much direct sun light, and keep soil moist using a fine spray.

PRICKING OUT

Seedlings are pricked out when the first pair of true leaves appear. Best results come from pricking out straight into individual peat or plastic pots. However, at a time of year when many plants need protection from sharp overnight spring frosts, space on greenhouse shelves and in cold frames is at a premium. Individual pots take up a great deal of space so it is often preferable to use a tray or flat. I usually prick out annuals into a deep tray filled to the brim with compost, with each seedling set well apart. I pot on the seedlings into a loam-based John Innes No 2, adding some sharp sand, in a ratio of about four parts compost to one part sand. Prize out the seedlings with a fork or widger and put each one in a prepared hole, handling as little as possible, holding only the leaves and not the fragile stems.

It is important to remember that during April and early May, greenhouses can heat up dangerously and seedlings will die unless shaded and sprayed. Harden the plants off by gradually reducing heat in the greenhouse and then housing the trays and pots

Marian Hill

HARDEN PLANTS OFF in a cold frame, if possible, before planting out in their permanent or summer sites. Leave off frame lids during the last few weeks before planting out. Young plants particularly dislike sudden changes in temperature. If you do not have cold frames for this, find a sheltered area for plants to be placed outside in pots in the final period before planting.

in cold frames well before planting time in the garden. Leave the lids off the cold frames during the last two weeks. Very young plants are, of course, also at risk from the climate when planted out. Where you live, and even the specific conditions in the micro-climate of your garden, will determine when it is safe to plant them. If your garden is subject to frosts in spring, take particular care to protect young plants during cold spells. Most of those seeds I grow - tobacco plants, cosmos, cleomes, cerinthes and salvias - are not planted out until the calendar has passed the 19th May, a magic date after which we seldom have a frost in our district. If not well hardened off, young plants can be killed by frost. Also, cold nights, even if temperatures do not fall below freezing, retard growth. Some annuals never really recover and perform well if they are stressed by cold nights after first being planted in permanent sites.

I find it difficult to go away from home during the period from late April to late May. Annuals seem to need almost twenty-four hour attention in the early growing stages, and certainly not abandoning over a weekend to possible scorching sun in the greenhouse before planting out, and/or freezing winds once in the ground. In reality, with help only twice a week, I have to take risks and often lose a few plants to the weather. When I was at Tintinhull, the National Trust property which I looked after for fourteen years, my husband and I never went away together during those vital weeks.

Most seeds are bought, of course, and grown in the same way. And seeds are often a gift. When I am in some exotic location I seldom refuse seed from plants I admire even if I know they are not suitable to the English climate or the heavy clay soil in my garden. I enjoy growing them in containers for a few years until they get too large. Amongst plants I have grown from seed are bomareas - climbing altroemerias from South America with delicate pinkish green hanging petals, Texan mountain laurel (*Sophora secundiflora*), a cousin of wisteria but naturally bush-like rather than a climber, and red yucca (*Hesperaloe parviflora*) also from the south west of North America. Sometimes, germinating exotic seeds is luck as often no information can be found on them in any of my books.

GROWING FROM CUTTINGS

Cuttings are one of the easiest ways to increase plant stock. This sort of vegetative propagation ensures an exact replica of the original plant. Shrubs and perennials with soft-growing tips and other softer-stemmed plants can be propagated from softwood cuttings once they are in spring growth. Take cuttings on a cool day, or in the morning or evening of a warm one, putting them immediately into a plastic collecting bag.

Tip-cuttings off softwood growth should normally include three leaf pairs and be at least 4cm (1½ in) long. They should not be taken from a flowering shoot. Use a sharp knife to cut just below a leaf node, which is where most of the root-forming nutrients collect. Trim off dead leaves and cut broad

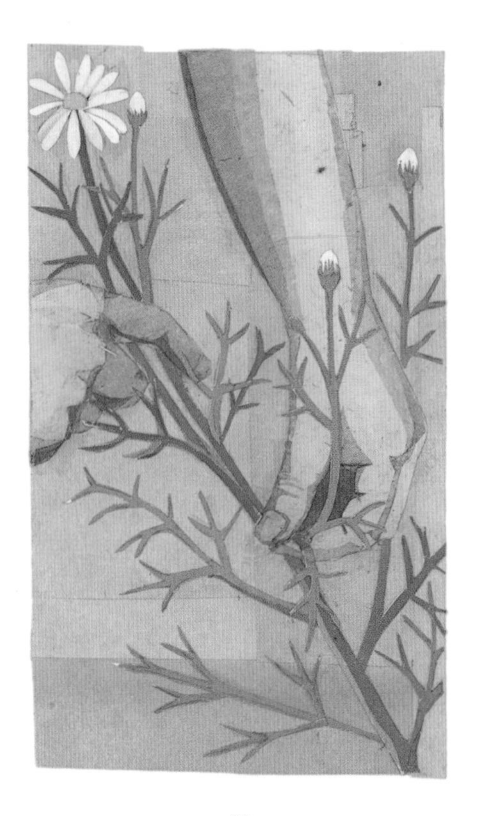

CUTTINGS ROOT MOST easily if they are pulled from a branch with a heel. Choose non-flowering stems if possible, or cut off any flowers or buds. Cuttings should be at least 4 cm (1½ in) long with at least two, preferably three, leaf pairs. Cut with a sharp knife just below a leaf node. Take cuttings on a cool day, or in the morning or evening if it is a warm one. Remove dead leaves and cut broad leaves in half to prevent loss of moisture.

leaves in half to prevent excess transpiration.

Later, from midsummer, a semi-ripe cutting, using the same method as for a tip cutting, can be taken just as the current year's growth is beginning to turn woody. At around the same time of year, semi-ripe cuttings from deciduous and evergreen shrubs and roses are nipped or pulled off as side shoots along with a heel from the main stem. Trim the heel with a knife before inserting it into the compost. Deciduous shrubs make shoots suitable for cutting from mid-summer, while evergreens root better from cuttings taken after September.

I have never regularly taken hardwood cuttings from fully-ripened wood. You need space outside for trenches, as the cuttings are planted directly into the ground for rooting and have to remain in such a site for nearly a year before transplanting or potting up.

Collect soft and semi-ripe cuttings into a plastic bag and get them into their rooting medium and container as soon as possible. Wilting and drying must be avoided. The compost I usually make for potting cuttings is a firm, moist mixture of peat and perlite. Others use peat and sand or even gravel, while some prefer a peat-free alternative but I don't find this very effective. Avoid using pots that are too small as they will dry out quickly – I generally use a pot of 75 mm (3 in) in diameter. Before planting, I dip all the ends of cuttings in a hormone rooting powder, which stimulates root growth. Then, using a sharp, pointed dibber, I make a planting hole before knocking off excess rooting powder and placing the cutting in its hole, firming the compost mixture tightly around the stem. I put six or more cuttings around the edge of each pot. These are potted up individually once they have made a satisfactory root system.

Twenty years ago I started using a mist propagator for rooting cuttings. This maintains a humid atmosphere above soil-warming cables. I became intoxicated by the ease of producing plants so quickly from semi-ripe wood taken in July or August. Mist systems should be turned off between December and February in a frost-free greenhouse. I learned over the years that many woody plants preferred a drier

LAVATERA, such as this *L. cachmiriana,* can be grown successfully from cuttings but choose non-flowering stems.

GET CUTTINGS INTO A FIRM potting medium, which I usually make from a moist mixture of peat and perlite, as soon as possible to avoid wilting. Use a dibber to make a hole and dip the ends of the cuttings first into a hormone rooting powder to stimulate growth. Insert at least one third of the stem of the cutting and make sure the compost fits tightly around and below the stem. Put six or more cuttings around the edge of each pot.

atmosphere, especially during the winter months. Grey and silver-leafed plants, particularly, dislike mist and are more easily rooted in an air-tight environment. The simplest form of equipment for this is a flowerpot covered with a polythene bag. A wooden box with a glass sheet or plastic film over it is equally effective as long as the air is kept moist and the potting medium does not dry out. Make sure the container is not left in bright sunlight.

Do not expose young cuttings to hot sun. If early cuttings have rooted before the end of September, they should be repotted. If not, leave them undisturbed until February, when longer days will again stimulate growth. Cuttings of tender plants are difficult to keep alive without glass but many of the hardiest kinds will survive in a sealed cold frame.

Many of the plants in my new garden are from cuttings or seeds of plants we grew at Tintinhull during the last years I was there. I feel quite sentimental about this provenance. I even have a young tree - a winged nut, *Pterocarya fraxinifolia* – which after five years is now five metres high and seems to enjoy the waterlogged clay in my garden. I have grown it from a cutting taken from a tree at Hadspen that was given to me in 1968. The Hadspen tree was grown from a cutting that originated from the magnificent specimen of the tree at Abbotsbury. I could have bought a much larger specimen from a nursery for my new garden but I like the feeling of continuity you get from knowing the parent plant.

DIVIDING PLANTS

Another way to make new plants from old, and perhaps the simplest and most basic of all, is by division. This normally works only with soft-stemmed herbaceous perennials. After a few years in situ, most established perennials can be dug up with a fork, keeping as much root as possible, and then split or cut up or teased apart to produce new plants. Apart from actually increasing the stock many of these plants benefit from being divided every few years; they will flower more prolifically.

Usually the central crowns are discarded and new plants are re-established from healthy growth found at the edge of the clump. Some tough plants such as hostas, campanulas, goats rue, phlox and asters are most quickly increased by division. The crowns of old plants which have become almost woody can be sliced with a spade or trowel, while younger specimens can be pulled apart with your hands or separated by pushing in two forks back to back and gradually applying pressure to split the crown or tease the roots apart. Abandon the oldest pieces and plant the rest straight back in the soil or pot up to be used later.

Sometimes if only a few new plants are required, as a gift or for a new site in the garden, it is easy to detach shoots with roots from the edge of a clump without disturbing the whole plant. Less vigorous than the parent, these clumps will need growing on in a pot, allowing them plenty of time to make a new root system before planting.

Perennials are best divided in autumn or spring. If

you extend these seasons into winter or summer you risk plants failing to get established before they face the extremes of heat and drought or cold and wet. On heavy clay spring division is best but, obviously, in very dry areas or with dry gravelly soil, the autumn will have its advantages.

Some plants have definite seasons when they make root growth and this will be a guide. Peonies need splitting up immediately after flowering, iris rhizomes are cut up in summer, while plants such as hellebores prefer early autumn.

TWO FORKS pushed back to back into the roots of a lifted plant provide a good way of dividing it. Gradually apply pressure to split the crown and pull the roots apart.

ACKNOWLEDGEMENTS

ILLUSTRATIONS by Marian Hill
DESIGNED by Roger Walton
PRODUCTION by Imago Publishing Ltd

Photograph of Penelope Hobhouse by Charles Hopkinson

First published in Great Britain by John Brown Publishing Ltd,
The New Boathouse, 136-142 Bramley Road, London
W10 6SR

ISBN 1-902212-290

Printed and bound in China for Imago